Mel Bay Presents

STUDENT'S MUSICAL DICTIONARY

by L. Dean Bye

TABLE OF CONTENTS

THE RUDIMENTS OF MUSIC

THE STAFF: Music is written on a STAFF consisting of FIVE LINES and FOUR SPACES. The lines and spaces are numbered upward as shown:

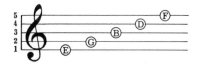

5TH LINE
4TH LINE — 4TH SPACE
3RD LINE — 3RD SPACE
2ND LINE — 2ND SPACE
1ST LINE — 1ST SPACE

THE LINES AND SPACES ARE NAMED AFTER LETTERS OF THE ALPHABET.

The LINES in the Treble Clef are named as follows:

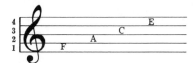

Fine
Does
Boy
Good

The letters may easily be remembered by the sentence - Every

The letter-names of the SPACES in the Treble Clef are:

They spell the word F-A-C-E

The musical alphabet has seven letters — A   B   C   D   E   F   G

The STAFF is divided into measures by vertical lines called BARS.

BAR   BAR

Heavy double bars
mark the end of a
section or strain
of music.

MEASURE   MEASURE   MEASURE

THE CLEF:

This sign is the treble or G Clef.

The second line of the treble clef is known as the G line. Many people call the treble clef the G clef because it circles around the G line.

NOTES:

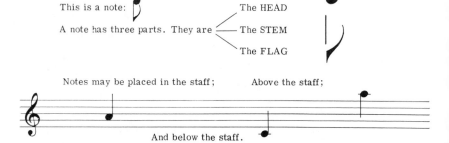

This is a note:

A note has three parts. They are
— The HEAD
— The STEM
— The FLAG

Notes may be placed in the staff;   Above the staff;

And below the staff.

A note will bear the name of the line or space it occupies on the staff. The location of a note in, above or below the staff will indicate the Pitch.

PITCH: The height or depth of a tone.

TONE: A musical sound.

TYPES OF NOTES

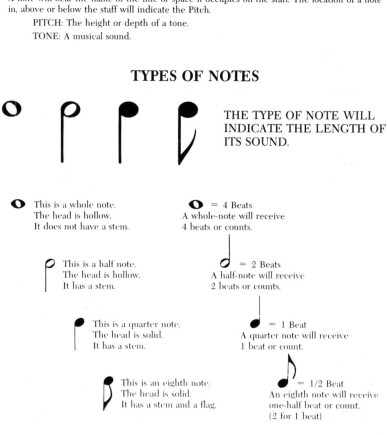

THE TYPE OF NOTE WILL INDICATE THE LENGTH OF ITS SOUND.

This is a whole note.
The head is hollow.
It does not have a stem.

= 4 Beats
A whole-note will receive 4 beats or counts.

This is a half note.
The head is hollow.
It has a stem.

= 2 Beats
A half-note will receive 2 beats or counts.

This is a quarter note.
The head is solid.
It has a stem.

= 1 Beat
A quarter note will receive 1 beat or count.

This is an eighth note.
The head is solid.
It has a stem and a flag.

= 1/2 Beat
An eighth note will receive one-half beat or count. (2 for 1 beat)

4

RESTS:

A REST is a sign used to designate a period of silence.

This period of silence will be of the same duration of time as the note to which it corresponds.

𝄾   This is an eighth rest.   **𝄽**   This is a quarter rest.

▬   This is a half rest. Note that it sits on the line.

▬   This is a whole rest. Note that it hangs down from the line.

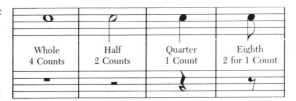

NOTES:

Whole 4 Counts	Half 2 Counts	Quarter 1 Count	Eighth 2 for 1 Count
▬	▬	𝄽	𝄾

RESTS:

THE TIME SIGNATURE

The above examples are common types of time signatures.

4
The top number indicates the number of beats per measure.

———

4
The bottom number indicates the type of note receiving one beat.

Example:

4
Beats per measure

———

4
A quarter-note receives one beat

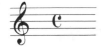
Signifies so called "common time" and is simply another way of designating 4/4 time.

LEDGER LINES:

When the pitch of a musical sound is below or above the staff, the notes are then placed on, or between, extra lines called LEDGER LINES.

They will be like this:

THE TIE

The TIE is a curved line between two notes of the same pitch.
The first note is played and held for the time duration of both.
The second note is not played but held.

Count 1 2 3 (1 2 3)

THE EIGHTH NOTE

An eighth note receives one-half beat. (One quarter note equals two eighth notes.)

An eighth note will have a head, stem, and flag. If two or more are in successive order, they may be connected by a bar. (See example.)

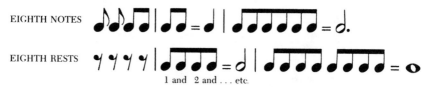

1 and 2 and . . . etc.

DOTTED QUARTER NOTES

A DOT after a note increases its value by ONE-HALF.

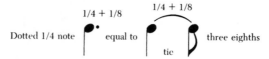

The count for the dotted quarter note is as follows:

Count: 1 2 & 3 4 &   1 2 & 3 4 &   1 2 & 3 4 &   1 2 & 3 4 &

6

ACCIDENTALS

♯ Sharp: raises pitch a half-step

♭ Flat: lowers pitch a half-step

𝄪 Double-Sharp: raises pitch two half-steps, or one whole-step

♭♭ Double-Flat: lowers pitch two half-steps or one whole-step

♮ Natural: cancels a sharp or a flat

BASIC TEMPO MARKINGS

Largo—Very slow and stately.
Largamente—Broadly. Quite slow.
Larghetto—Faster than *Largo,* but slow.
Grave—Seriously, solemn.
Lento—Slowly (often used temporarily)
Adagio—Slowly, very expressive
Andante—Tranquilly, but moving right along.
Andantino—Generally interpreted as slightly faster than *Andante.*

Moderato—Moderately. It is usually considered the medium point between the slowest and fastest markings.
Allegretto—Animated, but less than *Allegro*
Allegro—Lively, animated in movement.
Vivace—More rapidly than *Allegro.*
Presto—Very fast.
Prestissimo—The fastest tempo used.

PIANO KEYBOARD AND GRAND STAFF NOTATION

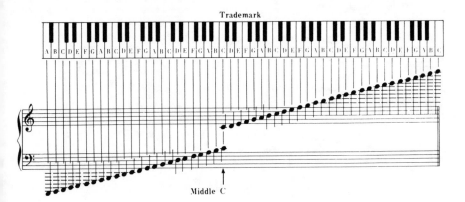

Trademark

Middle C

7

BUILDING A MAJOR SCALE

A major scale is a series of eight notes arranged in a pattern of whole steps and half steps.

C Major Scale

To construct a major scale we first start with the name of the scale *(Frequently called the Root or Tonic)*. With the C scale this would be the note "C." The rest of the scale would fall in line as follows:

C to D = Whole Step		G to A = Whole Step
D to E = Whole Step		A to B = Whole Step
E to F = 1/2 Step		B to C = 1/2 Step
F to G = Whole Step		

G MAJOR SCALE

To construct the G major scale, start with the note G, construct it as follows:

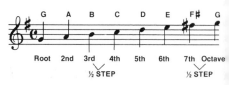

Notice that in order to make our formula work with the G scale we must sharp (#) the F. There must be a whole step between the 6th and 7th tones of the scale. In order to establish a whole step between E and F we must sharp the F.

SCALE TONES		DISTANCE FROM PRECEDING NOTE
ROOT	(C)	
2nd	(D)	Whole Step
3rd	(E)	Whole Step
4th	(F)	1/2 Step
5th	(G)	Whole Step
6th	(A)	Whole Step
7th	(B)	Whole Step
Octave	(C)	1/2 Step

WITH THE ABOVE FORMULA YOU CAN CONSTRUCT ANY MAJOR SCALE!

BUILDING MINOR SCALES
(also Jazz Scales and Modes)

Dorian
Formula:
Root - whole - 1/2 - whole - whole - whole - 1/2
step   step step   step   step   step

Pure Minor (Aeolian)
Formula: Find relative key-(up minor 3rd)-and begin your scale in that key on the 6th tone of that key. or: R-W-1/2-W-W-1/2-W-W.

Ascending Melodic Minor
Formula:
Root - W - 1/2 - W - W - W - W - 1/2

Harmonic Minor
Formula:
Root - W - 1/2 - W - W - 1/2 - b3rd Interval - 1/2

Phrygian
Formula:
Root - 1/2 - W - W - W - 1/2 - W - W

Blues Scale
Formula:
Root - b3rd Interval - W - 1/2 - 1/2 - b3rd Interval - W

8

CHORD BUILDING CHART*

Chord Type	Scale Degrees Used	Symbols
Major	Root, 3rd, 5th	Maj
Minor	Root, ♭3rd, 5th	mi, −, m
Diminished	Root, ♭3rd, ♭5th, ♭♭7th	dim, °
Augmented	Root, 3rd, ♯5th	+, aug.
Dominant Seventh	Root, 3rd, 5th, ♭7th	dom. 7, 7
Minor Seventh	Root, ♭3rd, 5th, ♭7th	−7, min 7
Major Seventh	Root, 3rd, 5th, maj. 7th	M7, ma 7
Major Sixth	Root, 3rd, 5th, 6th	M6, M6, 6
Minor Sixth	Root, ♭3rd, 5th, 6th	mi 6, −6
Seventh ♯5th	Root, 3rd, ♯5th, ♭7th	7^{+5}, $7^{\#5}$
Seventh ♭5th	Root, 3rd, ♭5th, ♭7th	7^{-5}, $7^{♭5}$
Major 7th ♭3rd	Root, ♭3rd, 5th, maj. 7th	Ma 7^{-3}
Minor 7th ♭5th	Root, ♭3rd, ♭5th, ♭7th	mi 7^{-5}, $−7^{♭5}$
Seventh Suspended 4th	Root, 4th, 5th, ♭7th	7 sus 4
Ninth	Root, 3rd, 5th, ♭7th, 9th	9
Minor Ninth	Root, ♭3rd, 5th, ♭7th, 9th	mi 9, −9
Major Ninth	Root, 3rd, 5th, maj. 7th, 9th	Ma 9
Ninth Augmented 5th	Root, 3rd, ♯5th, ♭7th, 9th	9^{+5}, $9^{\#5}$
Ninth Flatted 5th	Root, 3rd, ♭5th, ♭7th, 9th	9^{-5}, $9^{♭5}$
Seventh ♭9	Root, 3rd, 5th, ♭7th, ♭9th	7^{-9}, $7^{♭9}$
Augmented Ninth	Root, 3rd, 5th, ♭7th, ♯9th	9^{+}, 7^{+9}
9/6	Root, 3rd, 5th, 6th, 9th	$^{9}_{6}$, 6 add 9
Eleventh	Root, 3rd, 5th, ♭7th, 9th, 11th	11
Augmented Eleventh	Root, 3rd, 5th, ♭7th, 9th, ♯11th	11^{+}, 7 aug 11
Thirteenth	Root, 3rd, 5th, ♭7th, 9th, 11th, 13th	13
Thirteenth ♭9	Root, 3rd, 5th, ♭7th, ♭9th, 11th, 13th	$13^{♭9}$
Thirteenth ♭9♭5	Root, 3rd, ♭5th, ♭7th, ♭9th, 11th, 13th	$13^{♭9♭5}$
Half Diminished	Root, ♭3rd, ♭5th, ♭7th	Ø

*Note—To arrive at scale degrees above 1 octave (i.e., 9th, 11th. 13th) continue your scale up 2 octaves and keep numbering. The 2nd scale degree will be 9th tone as you begin your second octave.

KEY SIGNATURES

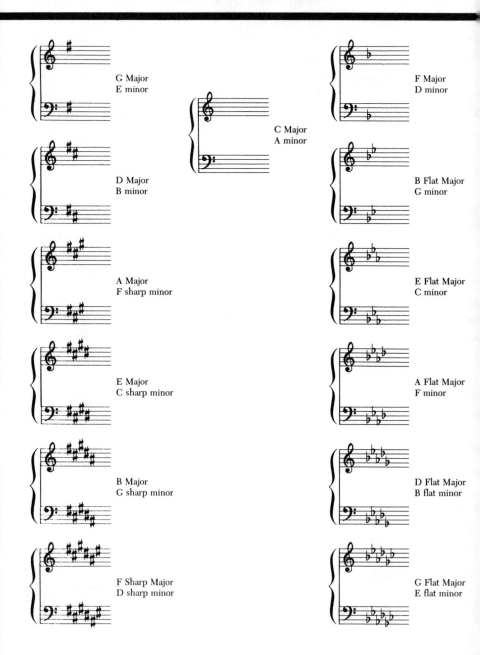

G Major
E minor

D Major
B minor

A Major
F sharp minor

E Major
C sharp minor

B Major
G sharp minor

F Sharp Major
D sharp minor

C Major
A minor

F Major
D minor

B Flat Major
G minor

E Flat Major
C minor

A Flat Major
F minor

D Flat Major
B flat minor

G Flat Major
E flat minor

FORM AND EXPRESSION MARKS

In order to read, write, or understand music, one must know all of the signs, words and abbreviations which are often referred to as the musical vocabulary. Many of these have been given on other pages, but most are included here.

1. A melody is a succession of single tones.

2. A chord is a combination of tones sounded together.

3. A triad is a three note chord.

Tones in a melody.

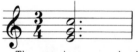
The same tones as a chord.

4. A phrase is a short musical thought -- a musical sentence. The phrase usually finishes on a note of longer duration, or at the end of a rhythmic pattern. A double bar does not necessarily mean the beginning or end of a phrase.

Example:

5. A period is a "complete musical thought" usually made up of two phrases.
Example:

6. A slur is a curved line drawn above or below groups of two or more notes. Usually this means that the notes are to be played or sung legato (Smoothly).

Example:

7. A tie is a curved line connecting two notes of the same letter name and pitch.

Example:

8. When sections or portions of a piece of music are to be repeated, various signs are used.

(A) D.C. (Da Capo) means to repeat from the beginning to the word Fine (the end).

Example:

(A B A)

(B) D.S. (Dal Segno) means to repeat from the Sign (𝄋) to the word Fine (the end).

Example:

(A B C B)

(C) Two dots before a double barline mean to return to the beginning or to another double bar followed by two dots.

Example:
(A A B B)

(D) First and second endings are often used after repetitions in music.

Example:
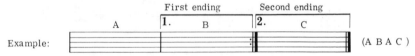
(A B A C)

9. DYNAMICS are indicated by words such as...

Pianissimo .... (*pp*) .... Very soft
Piano .... (*p*) .... Soft
Mezzo piano .... (*mp*) .... Medium soft
Mezzo forte .... (*mf*) .... Medium loud
Forte .... (*f*) .... loud
Fortissimo .... (*ff*) .... Very loud

10. The names of all scale degrees in a diatonic scale are:
First Degree - Tonic
Second Degree - Supertonic
Third Degree - Mediant
Fourth Degree - Subdominant
Fifth Degree - Dominant
Sixth Degree - Submediant
Seventh Degree - Leading Tone
Eighth Degree - Octave

ADDITIONAL EXPRESSION MARKS
AND ABBREVIATIONS

ad lib. - giving the performer liberty in matters of tempo and express-ion.

Accel. - Accelerando (increase speed or tempo)

$\overset{>}{\mathbf{P}}$ Accent - to stress or to emphasize

Accom. - Accompaniment

a tempo - resume strict time

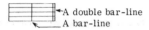 A double bar-line
A bar-line

V, ' - Breath marks

⊕ - Coda

⟍ or cresc. - crescendo
(get louder)

. - Dot
1) a dot placed after a note or rest increases the value one half. (Exp. ♩.)

2) a dot placed below or above a note indicates that the note should be played staccato. (Exp. ♩.)

⟋ or Dim. - Diminuendo
or Decresc. (get softer)

⌒ - a fermata or hold

Fine – the end

 (Subdivide) - in this case play four eighth notes.

Leg. - Legato (smoothly and connected)
meno - less
ped. - pedal
piu - more
rall. - rallentando (gradually slower)
repeat - a character indicating that certain measures or passages are to be sung or played twice.
(see previous page)

rit. - ritard or ritardando (gradually slower)

rubato - a flexibility of tempo - a quicken-ing and slowing of the tempo at the discretion of the performer or conductor.

sforzando (sfz) - a strong accent - imme-diately followed by piano (soft).

♯ ; ♭ ; ♮ - sharp; flat; natural

𝄪 - Double - Sharp ; raises the pitch two half-steps or one whole step.

♭♭ - Double - flat ; lowers the pitch two half steps or one whole step.

Sign - a note or character employed in music.

Spiccato - Italian for very detached. (usually used for string instru-ments.)

≣ - a staff

Suspension - the holding of a note in any chord into the chord which follows

♩ or ten. - tenuto - sustain for full value.

Triplet - ♩♩♩ - a group of three notes performed in the time of 2.

Tutti - All - Everyone sings or plays.

Unis. - Unison

Vamp - to improvise an accompaniment

8va. - 8 notes higher

Voce (It.) - the voice

Volume - The power (loudness or softness) of a voice or instrument
Whole step - two half steps or a major second

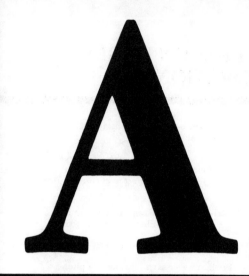

A — is the sixth note in the diatonic major scale of C. In the natural minor scale (the relative scale of C major) it is the first note.

A cappella (It.) — unaccompanied vocal music.

Accelerando (It.) — gradually increasing the rate of speed.

Accent — a strong emphasis upon a certain tone, chord, or beat.

Accessory notes — notes which are situated one degree above, and one degree below the principle note of a turn. The upper note of a trill is also called the accessory note.

Accidentals — sharps, flats, or naturals, which are not found in the key signature.

Accompaniment — a separate part or parts, either for voices or instruments which are subservient to a chief part. Some accompaniments may be omitted.

Accord —(Fr.) — a chord or consonance.

Accordion — a musical instrument which includes a keyboard for the right hand. The tone or sound is produced by the bellows which act upon metallic reeds.

Acoustics — the science of sound.

Adagietto (It.) — not as slowly as Adagio.

Adagio (It.) — slowly. Also, can be used as a name for a movement which is written this time. (slowly)

14

Adagio assai (It.) — very slowly.

Adagio cantabile (It). — very slow and sustained.

A dur (Ger.) — A Major

Agitato (It.) — a very restless and agitated style of playing or singing.

Agnus Dei (Lat.) — Lamb of God. One of the parts of a Mass.

Air — a short song or tune.

Al fine (It.) — to the end.

Alla breve — originally 4–2 meter. Now 4–4 time at a faster rate of speed and usually counted as 2–2.

Allargando (It.) — gradually growing louder and slower (broader).

Allegretto (It.) — slightly slower than Allegro.

Allegro (It.) — very quickly, although not as fast as Presto. The word is also used to describe a whole movement of a sonata or symphony.

    Allegro agitato (It.) — quite fast and in an excited manner.

    Allegro con brio (It.) — fast—with spirit.

    Allegro con moto (It.) — fast—with movement.

    Allegro con spirito (It.) — fast and spirited.

    Allegro moderato (It.) — moderately fast.

    Allegro molto (It.) — very fast.

    Allegro vivace (It.) — quite fast and in a vivacious manner.

Al segno (It.) — return to the sign.

Alto (It.) — originally this term was applied to high male voices. Presently it is generally used to refer to the lowest female voice.

Alto Clef — the C clef on the third line of the staff. This clef is used for the viola, alto trombone, and often, for the alto voice.

Andante (It.) — a movement in moderate time.

    Andante cantabile — slowly and sustained.

Andante con moto — slowly, but with some motion.

Andante grazioso — slowly and gracefully.

Andante maestoso — slowly and with a feeling of majesty.

Andante non troppo — moderately, but not too slowly.

Andante sostenuto — in a slow and sustained manner.

Andantino (It.) — the literal definition is—slightly slower than Andante. Present usage i generally faster than Andante.

Animato (It.) — animated and lively.

Anthem — a composition for voices, with or without instrumental accompaniment. The words usually come from the Bible or are religious in nature.

A póco — gradually or by degrees.

Appassionata (It.) — with intense feeling and emotion.

Appoggiatura (It.) — a grace note or a note of embellishment sometimes referred to as leaning note.

Arco (It.) — a violin bow.

Aria (It.) — an air or a song sung by a single voice either with or withou accompaniment.

    Aria buffa (It.) — a comic or humorous song.

    Aria cantabile (It.) — a song in a graceful or flowing style.

Arietta (It.) **Ariette** (Fr.) — a short song or melody.

Arioso (It.) — in a singing style or in the style of an Aria.

Arpeggiando (It.) — music played in the style of a harp (a musical imitation of a harp)

Arpeggio (It.) — a term applied to the notes of a chord played consecutively.

Arrangement — a selection or adaptation of a composition to instruments or voices fo which it was not originally written.

Articulation — distinct pronunciation.

A tempo (It.) — in time.

Attack — a firm and clear entry of voices or instruments at the beginning of a phrase.

Augmented — (1) an interval greater than perfect or major. (2) a theme or melody written in notes of greater value than in its original form.

Authentic cadence — the traditional name for a perfect cadence in which the harmony of the dominant is followed by that of the tonic.

Auxiliary scales — scales in relative keys.

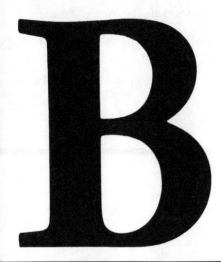

B — (1) the seventh note in the scale of C. (2) a major scale having five sharps in its key signature.

Bagpipe — an ancient wind-instrument of eastern origin now usually thought of as being an instrument from Scotland.

Ballad — a short simple song, designed to suit a popular audience. Usually the words are in a narrative or descriptive form.

Ballet (Fr.) — a theatrical representation of a story told in dancing and pantomime.

Banjo — a five-stringed instrument whose sound is reinforced by a parchment covered hoop.

Bar — a line drawn from the top to the bottom of a staff which shows the division of the time in a piece of music. A **bar** divides the music into measures.

Bar, double — heavy double bar lines drawn vertically through the staff usually designate the end of a section or a composition. Dots on either side of the double bar show that the preceding or following measures should be repeated.

Baritone — a male voice between the bass and tenor.

Barre (Fr.) — in lute or guitar playing, the stopping of several or of all of the strings with the left-hand forefinger.

Bass Clef — the F clef on the fourth line of the staff.

Basso (It.) — a bass singer.

Bassoon — a woodwind instrument of the oboe family with a range of three octaves. The bassoon forms the bass of woodwind instruments.

Basso ostinato (It.) — ground bass. A bass figure which is constantly repeated.

Bass Tuba — a brass instrument of very low pitch with a range of four octaves.

Bass Voice — the lowest male voice.

Baton (Fr.) — a conductor's stick or wand.

Beat — the rise or fall of the hand or **baton** in marking the divisions of time in music.

Bel canto (It.) — refers to singing in a pure, tender, legato style.

Bell — (1) the flaring end of the tube of various wind instruments. (2) a hollow instrument, set in vibration by a clapper inside or a hammer outside.

Benedictus (Lat.) — one of the parts of a Mass.

Berceuse (Fr.) — a lullaby or cradle song.

Binary — twofold—a form of two divisions, periods, or sections; two beats to a measure.

Boléro (Sp.) — a lively Spanish dance in 3/4 time.

Bourdon (Fr.) — an organ stop, usually consisting of stopped wooden pipes.

Bourrée (Fr.) — an old French dance generally in 2/4 or 2/2 time.

Bow — made of wood and horsehair and used to set the strings of a violin, viola, cello, or stringed bass in vibration.

Bowing — the art of using the bow; playing with the bow.

Brace — a mark connecting two or more staves together.

Bréve (It.) — (1) short. (2) the **Bréve** is now the longest note or double whole note.

Bridge — a piece of wood on instruments with a soundboard which performs a double duty of raising the strings and of terminating at one end their vibrating portion.

Brio (It.) — with fire; spirited.

Broken Chords — **Arpeggios.**

Bugle — a brass horn of straight or curved form most often used in military field music.

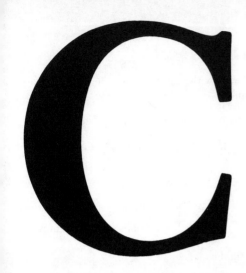

C — the first note of the natural scale.

Cadence (Fr.) — (1) the end of a phrase, either in the melody or the harmony. (2) The principle cadences in harmony are: the whole or authentic, the half, the interrupted and the plagal.

Cadenza (It.) — an ornamental passage usually introduced towards the end of the first and or last movements of a composition. It is generally of an impromptu character and designed to show the technical skills of a performer.

Canon — the composition in which each voice imitates exactly the melody sung or played by the preceding voice.

Cantabile (It.) — to perform in a singing and expressive style.

Cantata — a short work of several movements composed of arias, recitatives, an choruses.

Canticle — a song or hymn in honor of God

Canto (It.) — a song, chant, or melody. The highest vocal part in choral music.

Canzone (It.) — a song, folk song, or part-song in Madrigal style.

Caprice (Fr.) **Capriccio** (It.) — a whimsical, humorous composition in somewha irregular form.

Carillion — a set of bells arranged so they may be played by hand or by mechanical key

Carol — a song of praise usually applied to songs sung at Christmas time.

Castinet — a pair of small pieces of hard wood used to accompany Spanish dancing.

Catgut — the name used for the material of which many strings are made for musical instruments.

C Clef — the clef which shows the position of middle C. This clef is used for the soprano, alto, and tenor parts.

Celesta — an instrument consisting of metal bars which are struck with mallets through the medium of a keyboard.

Cello (It.) — an abbreviation of violincello.

Cembalo (It.) — a harpsichord.

Chaconne (Fr.) — an instrumental piece consisting of a series of variations above a ground base. (Also used to refer to a Spanish dance)

Chamber Music — compositions of instrumental music in the form of string quartets or quintets. Vocal or instrumental pieces suitable for performance in a small intimate setting.

Chanson (Fr.) — song

Chant — to recite musically.

Choir — the part of a cathedral or church set apart for the singers. Often used to refer to the singers themselves.

Choral — compositions for many voices. Music composed for the **Chorus** or **Choir.**

Chord — any combination of musical sounds.

Chord, common — a chord consisting of a fundamental note together with its third and fifth.

Chord, dominant — a chord found on the dominant of the key in which the music is written.

Chord, inverted — a chord, notes of which are so arranged that the root does not appear as the lowest note.

Chorus — (1) a body of singers. (2) the refrain of a song.

Chromatic — (1) proceeding by half steps. (2) any music or chord containing notes which do not belong to the diatonic scale.

21

Church modes — plain song or chant (see Gregorian chant).

Circle of fifths — a method of modulation, from dominant to dominant, which takes one through all the scales, back to the point where he started.

Clarinet — a full-toned wind instrument often made of wood with a single reed mouthpiece.

Classical music — music of the highest order. Music whose form and style has been accepted as worthy of performance and as suitable as a model to other composers.

Clavichord — a stringed instrument from the Middle Ages which is the forerunner of the harpsichord and piano.

Clavier (Ger.) — the German name for harpsichords, clavichords, and pianos.

Clef — the character used to determine the name and pitch of the notes on the staff on which it appears.

Coda (It.) — the end.

Codetta (It.) — a short **Coda.**

Common Time — a term sometimes used to refer to a piece of music with two beats in a bar or any multiple of two beats in a bar. Common time is of two kinds; simple and compound.

Concert — a public performance of music by either vocal or instrumental musicians.

Concertina — (It.) a small instrument similar to the accordion with hexagonal sound boxes rather than oblong ones.

Concert Master — the chief violinist of an orchestra and the leader of the violins.

Concerto (It.) — a composition written to display a solo instrument, usually with orchestral accompaniment.

Conductor — the director or leader of an orchestra or chorus.

Consecutive fifths — two or more perfect fifths, immediately following one another in similar motion.

Conservatory — a school of music, in which every branch of musical art is taught.

Console — the keyboard (including pedals and stops) of an organ.

Consonance — sounds, which when played together, are agreeable and satisfactory to the ear.

Contralto (It.) — the lowest female voice (usually called alto).

Contrary motion — melodic or harmonic motion in opposite directions.

Cornet — a modern brass instrument having valves or pistons. Similar in many ways to the trumpet.

Counterpoint — **Point against point** — or melody against melody. The term "Counterpoint" in its broadest sense is defined as the art of adding one or more additional melodies to a given melody.

Courante (Fr.) — an old French dance in 3/2 time.

Credo (Lat.) — the creed. One of the parts in the Mass.

Crescendo (It.) — swelling or increasing the force of sound.

Cymbals — circular brass plates which vibrate after being crashed together.

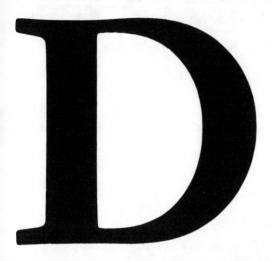

D — (1) the second note in the diatonic scale of C. (2) the key which has two sharps in its key signature.

Da capo (It.) — from the beginning.

Da capo al fíne (It.) — return to the beginning and conclude at the word fíne.

Da capo al segno (It.) — return to the beginning and play to the sign, after which play the **Coda**.

D.C. — the initials of **Da capo**.

De crescendo (It.) — to gradually decrease in volume.

Development — the elaboration on a given theme.

Diatonic — proceeding in the order of the degrees of the natural scale (the standard major or minor scale).

Diminished — made less. For example: diminished intervals are those made less than minor.

Diminuendo (It.) — to become softer.

Discord — a combination of dissonant sounds.

Dissonance — a discord. Augmented and diminished intervals, seconds, sevenths, and ninths, are called dissonances.

Divertimento (lt.) — any of various light melodic instrumental compositions in several movements.

Dolce (lt.) — sweetly and delicately.

Dominant — the name applied to the fifth note of the scale.

Dominant chord — a chord built on the dominant or fifth note of the scale.

Dot — a dot under a note means that that note should be played staccato. A dot after a note prolongs its time value by half.

Double bar — two vertical lines drawn through the staff at the end of a section, movement, or the entire composition.

Double bass — the largest and lowest pitched instrument played with the bow.

Double flat — a character which lowers a tone two half steps.

Double reed — the mouthpiece of the oboe and bassoon, etc. formed by joining two pieces of cane together.

Double sharp — a character which raises a tone two half steps.

Double stopping — the stopping of two strings simultaneously with the fingers when playing the violin.

Double time — a time in which every measure is composed of two equal parts.

Duet — a composition for two voices or instruments or for two performers on one instrument.

Duple — double. Two beats in the measure.

Dynamics — refers to expression in music and to the different degrees of power to be given to the notes.

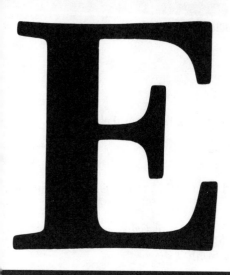

E — (1) in the scale of C the third note. (2) the major key which has four sharps in its key signature.

Embellishment — the ornaments of melody; such as trills, turns, mordent, etc.

Embouchure (Fr.) — (1) the mouthpiece of a wind instrument. (2) the position of the mouth and lips of the player.

Enharmonic — (1) having intervals less than a semi-tone. (2) the **Enharmonic** scale is one which contains intervals less than a semi-tone.

Ensemble (Fr.) — together. The union of the whole company of performers in either vocal or instrumental music.

Episode — the parts of a fugue between the repetitions of the main theme.

Expressivo (It.) — with expression.

Etude (Fr.) — a study or exercise.

Expression — the act of rendering music so that it displays feelings and emotions. This is as opposed to the mere mechanical production of sound.

F — (1) in the diatonic scale of C, the fourth note. (2) the name of the major scale which has one flat in its key signature.

f — the abbreviation of Forte; ff, fortissimo; and fff, fortississimo.

Falsetto (It.) — the artificial high tones of the voice usually used to refer to the male "head-voice".

Fanfare — a trumpet flourish or trumpet call.

Fantasia (It.) — a selection in which the composer yields to his imagination. A composition which is not in any regular form.

Fermata (It.) — a Hold.

Fife —a small shrill musical instrument of the flute type.

Fifth — an interval measuring five diatonic degrees. It also refers to the fifth degree in any diatonic scale.

Figure — a form of melody or accompaniment maintained throughout the phrase where it appears.

Finale (It.) — the closing number of the last movement in a large musical composition.

Fine (It.) — the end.

Fingering — (1) the method of applying fingers to the keys, strings, or holes of various instruments. (2) the figures written on the musical page to show the performer which finger to use in playing a note.

Flat — the sign which lowers the pitch of the note one semi-tone.

Flute — an extremely well-known wind instrument made either of wood or of metal, consisting of a tube closed at one end with both holes and keys to be depressed or covered by the fingers, thus altering the pitch.

Form — the melodic and rhythmic order in which musical ideas are presented.

Forte — (It.) — loudly.

Fortissimo (It.) — extremely loud.

Forzando (It.) — with emphasis or to place musical accents upon specified notes or passages.

Fourth — an interval of four notes.

Frets — small strips of wood, ivory, or metal placed upon the fingerboard of certain string instruments (i.e. guitars or banjos) to regulate the pitch of the notes produced.

Fugue — a polyphonic composition constructed on one or more short themes which are introduced from time to time with various contrapuntal devices.

Fundamental — the root on which any chord is built.

G — (1) the fifth note of the normal scale of C. (2) a key note of a major scale which has one sharp in its key signature.

Galop (Fr.) — a lively dance in 2/4 time.

Gavotte (Fr.) — an elegant and graceful French dance of even rhythm.

G Clef — the Treble Clef; a character representing the letter G turns on the second line of the staff (the G Line).

German Sixth — a name given to a chord composed of a major third, a perfect fifth, and an augmented sixth.

Gigue (Fr.) — a jig— a very lively type of French dance.

Glissando (It.) — (1) on bowed-instruments, it is a flowing, unaccented execution of a passage. (2) on the piano, a rapid scale-effect obtained by sliding a fingernail over the key.

Glockenspiel (Ger.) — a set of small bars of polished steel, which are struck with a mallet.

Gloria (Lat.) — a section of the Mass also referred to as the Gloria in Excelsis.

Grace-note — ornamental notes and embellishments, either written in by the composer or added by the performer.

Grand — large, great, full, or complete.

29

Grandioso (It.) — grand, noble.

Grave (It.) — the slowest tempo in music.

Great Octave — the notes lying between C and B inclusive.

Gregorian Chant — plain chant—a style of choral music according to the celebrated church modes introduced by Pope Gregory in the sixth century.

Grosso (It.) — great, grand, full.

Ground Bass — a constantly repeated bass passage of four or eight bars.

Guitar — a plucked stringed instrument of great resonance. The instrument is universally known and popular and was originally intended for accompaniment only. In modern times, it has become a widely used solo instrument.

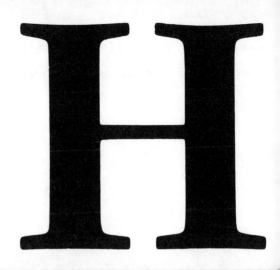

Habanera — a slow Spanish dance in 3/4 or 6/8 time.

Half-note — a note half the duration of a whole note.

Half-rest — a rest half the duration of a whole rest.

Harmonica — a musical instrument which is also called a mouth organ. The modern harmonica is a small hand-held reed instrument.

Harmonic modulation — a change in the harmony from one key to another.

Harmonics — overtones.

Harmonic Scale — the scale formed by a series of natural harmonies.

Harmony — (1) the art of combining tones into chords. (2) the agreement or consonance of two or more spontaneous sounds.

Harp — a stringed instrument of ancient origin, consisting of a triangular frame with strings which are played with the fingers.

Harpsichord — an instrument used extensively before the invention of the piano. The strings in a harpsichord are plucked by quills.

Hold — a character which indicates that a note or rest is to be prolonged (see **Fermata**).

Homophony — the opposite of polyphony. In modern times, a style in which one melody is supported by chords.

Horn — a metal wind instrument.

Hymn — a religious or sacred song usually used in Christian worship.

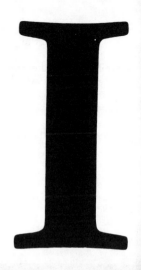

Imitation — the repetition of a motive, phrase, or theme.

Impresario — a term applied by Italians to the manager or conductor of an opera or a concert.

Impromptu (Fr.) — a composition of an extemporaneous character.

Improvisation — the art of singing or playing music without preparation. Extemporaneous performance.

Improvise — to create on the spur of the moment.

Incidental music — descriptive music, generally orchestral, accompanying a play.

Instrument — any mechanical contrivance for the production of musical sound.

Instrumentation — (1) the art of using several musical instruments in combination. (2) the act of writing for an orchestra or band.

In tempo (It.) — in strict time.

Interlude — a short piece played between longer musical sections, acts, or religious services.

Intermezzo — a short piece or interlude.

Interval — the difference in pitch between two simultaneous tones.

Intonation — a word referring to the proper tonal emission either vocal or instrumental. The producing of any required note in exact tune.

Introduction — the preliminary movement of a composition which prepares the ear for the movements which are to follow.

Invention — a short piece in free contrapuntal style.

Inversion — a change of position with respect to intervals and chords.

Jew's harp — a small instrument of brass or steel held between the lips, with a thin, vibrating tongue of metal, twitched by the forefinger.

Jig — a lively dance.

Just — a term often applied to consonant intervals.

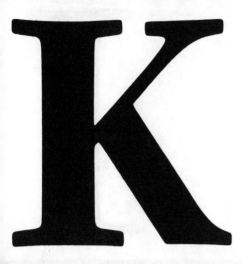

Kanon (Ger.) — a **Canon.**

Kettle drum — an orchestral percussion instrument consisting of a hollow brass or copper shell over which a head is stretched.

Key — (1) a series of tones forming any given major or minor scale. (2) a finger or foot lever for producing tones in a piano or organ.

Keyboard — the whole series of levers for producing tones in a piano or organ.

Kyrie eleison (Lat.) — the first movement in the Mass.

Langsam (Ger.) — slow.

Largamente (It.) — broadly and/or slowly.

Larghetto (It.) — rather slow, but not as slow as **Largo**.

Largo (It.) — very slow.

Larynx — the organ situated at the top of the windpipe, by which we produce vocal sound.

Leading-note — the seventh degree of an ascending scale.

Ledger lines — short additional lines which are drawn above or below the staff.

Legato (It.) — in a smooth and connected manner.

Leit motif (Ger.) — a theme or phrase associated with a character, thought, or action in a modern music drama. German composer, Richard Wagner, used the Leit motif extensively in his operas.

Lento (It.) — slow.

Libretto (It.) — the text of an opera or an oratorio.

Lied (Ger.) — a song or ballad.

Loud pedal — the right pedal on a piano which lifts the dampers from the strings.

Lute — an ancient stringed instrument—a predecessor of the guitar.

Lyre — one of the most ancient stringed instruments similar to a harp.

Lyric — poetry written to be set to music.

M.M. — the abbreviation for Maelzel's Metronome.

Madrigal — an unaccompanied, polyphonic, secular composition.

Maestoso (It.) — majestically and with dignity.

Major — **greater,** with respect to intervals and scales.

Major scale — the scale in which the half-steps fall between the third and fourth and the seventh and eighth tones both in ascending and descending order.

Mandolin — a pear-shaped instrument of the lute family with four strings. It is usually tuned like a violin.

Marcato (It.) — with marked emphasis.

March — a composition with strongly marked rhythm. It is generally written in 2/4 time.

Marimba — a percussion instrument made of a series of graduated pieces of hard wood, which are struck with hammers.

Marks of Expression — the words or signs used in music to regulate degrees of accent, time, or tone.

Mass (Lat.) — in the Roman Catholic and Anglican churches, the celebration of the Eucharist or Lord's Supper.

Mazurka — a lively Polish dance in 3/8 or 3/4 time.

Measure — the portion of the staff enclosed between two barlines.

Melodrama — a musical drama in which the dialogue is recited to a musical accompaniment.

Melody — a succession of tones rhythmically and symetrically arranged to produce a pleasing effect.

Meno (It.) — less.

Meno mosso (It.) — less movement; slower.

Menuet (Fr.) — a slow dance in 3/4 time (a minuet).

Metronome — a mechanical device for determining the time value of the beat.

Mezzo (It.) — half or medium.

Mezzo Forte (It.) half loud.

Mezzo Piano (It.) — half soft.

Mezzo Soprano (It.) — a voice lower in range than a soprano and higher than a contralto.

Middle C — the note which appears in the exact middle of the Grand Staff. It lies on the first ledger line above the Bass Staff and the first ledger line below the Treble Staff.

Minor (Lat.) — less or smaller.

Minor Scale — a scale formed by starting on the sixth degree of the major scale; also by lowering the third and sixth degrees of a given major scale, one half-step.

Minuet (see Menuet)

Mode —(1) a scale in Greek and early Ecclesiastical music. (2) in modern usage it is used with the terms major or minor—such as major mode or minor mode.

Moderato (It.) — moderately.

Modulation — a change of key. The gradual movement from one key to another by a succession of chords.

Molto (It.) — very much.

Monody — a song for a single voice.

Monotone — to sing or recite words on a single note without changing pitch.

Mordent — a group of two or more grace notes played rapidly before a principle note.

Motet (or Motete) — a sacred composition for several voices.

Motive — a musical subject proposed for development.

Mouthpiece — the part of a wind instrument which is put into the mouth of the performer or against the performer's lips.

Movement — (1) motion of the melody or part. (2) a division or portion of an extended composition.

Mute — (1) a small contrivance of wood or metal placed on the bridge of a stringed instrument to dampen the sound. (2) a pear-shaped contrivance placed in the bell of a brass instrument to dampen its sound.

Nacht-musik (Ger.) — Night music.

Natural — a character used to cancel a sharp or a flat.

Neapolitan Sixth — a chord occurring on the fourth degree of the scale consisting of a minor third and a minor sixth.

Neck — the part of stringed instruments such as violins or guitars which lies between the pegbox and the body of the instrument.

Neumes — musical notation used in early Middle Ages. Forerunner of notes.

Ninth — the interval of an Octave plus a major or minor Second.

Nocturne (Fr.) — a piece of "program" literature; often of a romantic character.

Nomenclature — in music, this term applies to the various signs employed to represent pitch, sound, time, pace, and expression.

Non troppó (It.) — not too much.

Notation — the various signs used to represent music on the printed page; such as staves, clefs, notes, rests, etc.

Note — a printed sign which shows us the relative duration and pitch of a sound.

Obligato — an additional part to a vocal or instrumental solo often lying above the melody.

Oboe (It.) — a double reed woodwind instrument.

Octave — eight notes above or below a given note; the interval of an eighth.

Open harmony — chords formed by as equidistant a disposition of the parts as possible.

Open strings — strings which produce the sounds assigned to them on a particular instrument. Strings whose pitch is unaltered by the "stopping" with the pressure of the finger.

Opera — musical drama; an extended musical work for voices and instruments,which is produced with costumes, scenery, and dramatic effects.

Operetta — a little opera.

Opus (Lat.) — work; extensively used by composers to number the order in which their compositions were written.

Oratorio (It.) — a religious composition similar to an opera which consists of solos, recititives, and choruses but performed without the aid of costumes, scenery, and dramatic action.

Orchestra — a body of performers on string, woodwind, brass, and percussion instruments. The modern symphony orchestra consists of from 60 to 120 performers.

Orchestration — the art of composing or arranging music for an orchestra.

Overtones — tones produced by a vibrating body above its fundamental tone.

Overture — an introductory selection, often a prelude to an opera or an oratorio.

P — abbreviation used for the dynamic marking, piano (small p); pp, pianissimo.

Parallel intervals — intervals passing in parallel parts in the same direction.

Parallel motion — the movement of two or more parts at fixed intervals.

Passacaglia (It.) — an ancient dance in triple time.

Passage — (1) a musical phrase. (2) a musical figure.

Passing Note — notes which do not belong to the harmony.

Pastoral — "program" music pertaining to or representing rural life.

Pause (Fr.) — a rest or pause.

Pedal — a mechanism controlled by the foot.

Pentatonic scale — the name given to the ancient scale formed by the black keys of the piano.

Percussion — any instrument that is struck (i.e. a drum, a bell, cymbals, etc.).

Period — a complete musical sentence.

Phrase — part of a musical sentence.

Phrasing — dividing musical sentences into rhythmical sections; usually indicated by using a slur.

Pianissimo (It.) — as softly as possible.

Piano (It.) — softly.

Piano forte (It.) — the complete name for a stringed instrument with a keyboard on which the tones are produced by felt hammers striking the strings.

Piccolo (It.) — (1) small or little. (2) a small woodwind instrument similar to the flute.

Pitch — the height or depth of a tone.

Piu (It.) — more.

Piu mosso (It.) — more motion or quicker.

Pizzicato (It.) — the strings are to be plucked, which produces a staccato effect.

Plagal cadence — the final tonic chord preceded by the subdominant.

Plain chant or **Plain-song** — the names given to old ecclesiastical chants when it was in its most simple state and without harmony. Often used interchangeably with the name Gregorian chant.

Plectrum (Lat.) — a quill used to pluck the strings on the harpsichord or other string instruments.

Poco (It.) — a little.

Poco a poco (It.) — little by little.

Polka — a Bohemian dance in 2/4 time.

Polonaise — a stately Polish dance in 3/4 time.

Polyphonic or **Polyphony** — many voiced or the blending of several independent melodies.

Portamento (It.) — gliding from one note to another.

Position — (1) the position of a chord is the same as the disposition of its parts. (2) a "position" on a violin or any other stringed instrument means to use the fingers in other than their normal place.

PP — the abbreviation for pianissimo.

Prelude — a musical introduction to a composition.

Prestissimo (It.) — very quickly.

Presto (It.) — quickly; faster than allegro.

Prima or **Primo** (It.) — first.

Primary accent — the accent beginning a measure.

Primary triad — one of the three fundamental triads of any key (I, IV, V).

Prime (Ger.) — the first note of the scale.

Progression — the movement from note to note or from chord to chord.

Psalm — a sacred song or hymn.

Psaltery — a very ancient string instrument mentioned in the Old Testament.

47

Quarter-note — a note one-fourth the value of a whole note.

Quarter-rest — a rest equal in time-value to a quarter note.

Quartet — an instrumental or vocal composition for four performers.

Quintet — a composition for five solo performers.

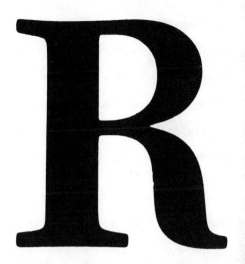

Rallentando (It.) — gradually slower.

Rapidamente (It.) — quickly/rapidly.

Recitative — a type of musical declamation.

Reed — a thin strip of cane or wood which when set in vibration produces a musical sound.

Reel — a lively peasant dance.

Refrain — the chorus at the end of every verse of some songs.

Related — a term applied to those chords or keys which permit an easy and natural transition from one to the other.

Repeat — a sign which indicates that certain measures or passages are to be performed twice.

Reprise (Fr.) — the chorus of a song.

Requiem (Lat.) — the Mass for the Dead.

Resin — rosin.

Resolution — the movement of a dissonant sound to a consonant sound.

Rests — signs which indicate silence of the same duration as the notes for which they stand.

Rhapsodie/Rhapsody — a free and often brilliant composition of irregular form.

Rhythm — the division of musical ideas or sentences into regular metrical portions.

Rigaudon (Fr.) — a lively French dance.

Rit — abbreviation of Ritardando.

Ritardando (It.) — retarding—delaying the time gradually.

Rondo (It.) — a composition which consists of a prominent theme alternating with other contrasting themes.

Root — the fundamental note of any chord.

Rosin — a gum, which, when properly prepared is used to rub over the hair of a bow.

Round — a form of canon in which several voices enter at staggered intervals, but sing the same melody.

Roundelay — a poem, certain lines of which are repeated.

Rubato (It.)—taking certain liberties with note duration—some notes are held slightly longer and some notes are held slightly shorter than their exact value.

Saraband (Eng.) — a dance in slow 3/4 or 3/2 time, said to be of Spanish origin.

Saxophone — a metal woodwind instrument with single reed mouthpiece.

Scale — a series of consecutive tones proceeding by half-steps (chromatic) or half-steps and whole steps (major) or by half-steps, whole steps, with occasional step and a half (minor).

Scherzando (It.) — playful and lively.

Scherzo (It.) — joke. A piece of music of a playful character.

Schnell (Ger.) — quickly.

Schottische — a rather slow dance in 2/4 time.

Score — the whole instrumental or vocal parts of a composition written on separate staves and placed under each other.

Second — an interval measuring two diatonic degrees.

Secondary chords — chords built on II, III, VI, or VII.

Secondo (It.) — second.

Section — a complete, but not an independent musical idea. Also refers to a family of instruments within the orchestra.

Segno (It.) — a sign. Directs the performer to turn back and repeat from the place marked by the sign.

Segue (It.) — in a similar manner. Go on.

Sehr (Ger.) — very much.

Sempre (It.) — always or continually.

Septet — a composition for seven voices or instruments.

Septuplet — a group of seven equal notes to be performed in the same time of four or six.

Sequence — the recurrence of a melodic motif.

Serenade — night music; an evening concert.

Serioso (It.) — gravely or seriously.

Seventh — an interval measuring seven diatonic degrees.

Seventh chord — a chord composed of a root, its third, fifth, and seventh.

Sextet — a composition for six voices or instruments.

Sextuplet (Lat.) — a group of six notes, to be played in the time of four.

Sf or **Sfz** — abbreviations for Sforzando.

Sforzando (It.) — with sudden emphasis.

Sharp — the sign which raises the pitch of a note one half step.

Sign — a note or character employed in printed music.

Signature — the signs, such as sharps, flats, or fractional figures, placed at the beginning of a piece of music. There are two kinds of signatures—the time signature and the key signature.

Simile (It.) — in the same manner or similarly.

Sinfonia (It.) — symphony.

Sixteenth-note — a note one half the length of an eighth note.

Sixteenth-rest — a pause equal in duration to a sixteenth note.

Sixth — an interval measuring six diatonic degrees.

Skip — a melodic progression from any note to another which is at a greater interval than one degree.

Slide — (1) a movable tube in the trombone. (2) to pass from one note to another without any cessation of sound.

Slur — a curved line placed over notes directing that they be played legato.

Solfeggio (It.) — a vocal exercise.

Solo (It.) — alone.

Sonata (It.) — an extended piano composition with several movements.

Sonatina (It.) — a short sonata.

Song — a short poem intended for music or a musical setting of a short poem.

Soprano (It.) — the highest kind of female voice.

Sostenuto (It.) — sustaining the tone.

Sotto (It.) — under or below.

Sotto voce (It.) — softly; as in an undertone.

Space — in the staff, the interval between the lines or the ledger lines.

Spiccato (It.) — detached.

Spirito, con (It.) — with spirit and energy.

Staccato (It.) — in a crisp and detached manner.

Staff or Stave — the five parallel lines used in modern musical notation.

Stem — the line attached to a note-head.

Step — a melodic progression of a second.

Stretta (It.) — a closing passage or coda in quicker tempo than the one preceding.

Stretto (It.) — hurried. Also, a division in a fugue, in which subject and answer follow in such quick succession that they overlap.

String — prepared wire, silk, or catgut, which is used for musical instruments.

String Quartet — a composition in four parts for two violins, viola, and cello.

Study — a composition in the style of an exercise.

Sub (Lat.) — under or below.

Subdominant — the fourth degree of a scale.

Subito (It.) — suddenly; at once.

Subject — a melody or theme.

Suite (Fr.) — a set or series of movements.

Super (Lat.) — above or over.

Super-tonic — the second degree of the scale.

Suspension — the holding or prolonging of a note in any chord into the chord which follows.

Sustained Note — a name given to prolonged notes.

Symphony — a large composition of several movements for a full orchestra. Also, often used to refer to the orchestra itself.

Symphonic poem — a form of orchestral composition originated by Liszt and developed by other romantic composers. It is a piece of program music and is descriptive in character.

Syncopation — the shifting of an accent from a strong beat to a weak beat.

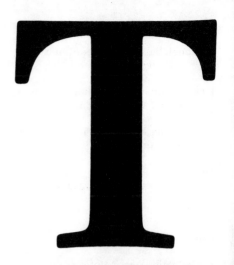

Tablature (Fr.) — a system of notation used for fretted instruments such as guitar and banjo.

Tacet (Lat.) — the silent tambourine. A percussion instrument formed of a hoop of wood or metal over which is stretched a piece of skin. The sides of the hoop are pierced with holes into which are inserted metal jingles.

Tarantella (It.) — a rapid Italian dance.

Tempo (It.) — rate of movement or speed.

Tempo-mark — a word or phrase indicating the rate of speed for a piece of music.

Ten. — abbreviation of "tenuto."

Tenor — the highest male voice.

Tenor-clef — the C-clef on the fourth line.

Tenuto (It.) — held or sustained.

Ternary — progressing by threes.

Tessitura (It.) — the range from lowest to highest tone.

Tetrachord — a series of four consecutive notes.

Theme — (1) the subject of a fugue. (2) simple melody on which variations are made.

Theory of Music — the science of music.

Thorough bass or Basso continuo — a system of harmony developed in the 1600's which i indicated by a figured bass.

Tie — a curved line joining two notes of the same pitch and adding the duration of the second note to the first.

Time — the division of musical phrases into portions marked by the regular return o an accent.

Toccata (It.) — a brilliant composition for piano or organ designed to demonstrate the expertise of the performer.

Tonality — pertaining to the key.

Tone — (1) sound. (2) often refers to a Gregorian chant.

Tonic — the keynote of a scale.

Tonic Chord — the common chord of which the tonic is the root.

Tranquillo (It.) — tranquilly or quietly.

Transcription — the arrangement of a composition for some voice or instrument other than that for which it was originally written.

Transient — passing.

Transition — modulation, a passing note.

Transpose — to perform or write out a composition in a different key.

Transposing instruments — instruments which are in any other key than C. The actual sound or key produced depends upon the instrument itself.

Treble — the highest voice or part; also refers to the G-clef.

Tremolo (It.) — a quivering or fluttering.

Triad — a chord of three notes.

Triangle — a percussion instrument made of a steel rod bent into a three-sided shape and struck with a small metal bar.

Trill (Fr.) — a shake, usually produced by the rapid alteration of two notes.

Trio (It.) — (1) a piece for three voices. (2) a section of a minuet, march, etc.

riplet — a group of three notes performed in the time of two.

rombone — a brass wind-instrument which consists of two tubes, sliding in and out of the other.

roubadours — a type of poet and musician in medieval France who wandered around the country singing for hire.

rumpet — a brass wind-instrument with valves.

uba — a valved brass instrument of very low pitch.

une — (1) a simple melody. (2) intonation.

uning — the adjustment of an instrument to a recognized pitch.

urn — an embellishment consisting of a group of rapid notes connecting one principle note with another.

utti (It.) — everyone.

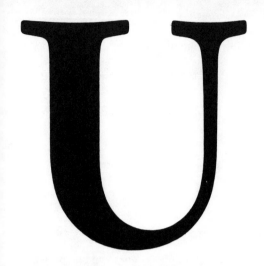

Unison — singing exactly the same note or an octave for mixed voices or instruments.

Un poco (It.) — a little.

Upbeat — an unaccented beat.

Valse (Fr.) — waltz.

Valve — in brass instruments, a device which shortens or lengthens the brass tubing to sound the semitones and tones between the natural open harmonics.

Vamp — to improvise an accompaniment.

Variation — certain modifications with regard to the time, tune, and harmony of a theme.

Verse — a separate stanza of a song or a ballad. It also sometimes refers to the text.

Vibrato (It.) — a tremulous quality of tone.

Viol — an instrument similar to the violin, but a little larger and with six strings.

Viola (It.) — an orchestral stringed instrument similar to the violin, but larger. Music for this instrument is written in the alto clef.

Violin — the leading stringed instrument in the orchestra composed of a gracefully shaped wooden box with four strings. It is most often played by means of a bow.

Violoncello (It.) — a four-stringed bowed instrument shaped like a violin, but held, while playing, between the knees.

Virginal — an early stringed instrument played by means of a keyboard like the piano.

Virtuoso (It.) — a great instrumental or vocal artist.

Vivace (It.) — very lively.

Vocal — music intended to be sung.

Vocalization — the manner of warming the vocal apparatus usually by prescribed exercises.

Voce (It.) — the voice.

Voice — the sounds produced by the human organs of speech. Also, may be used to refer to one of the parts in a polyphonic composition.

Volume — a term which refers to the power and quality of the tone of a voice or an instrument.

Voluntary — an organ solo played before, during, or after any part of the worship service of the Church.

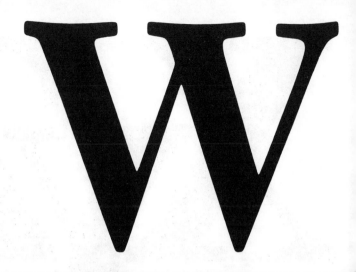

Waltz or Valse (Fr.) — a dance said to have originated in Bohemia—always with three beats to the measure. "Classical Waltzes" are compositions in waltz-form but are intended for performance.

Whole note — the longest note in value used in modern notation.

Whole rest — a pause equal in length to a whole note.

Whole step — a major second.

Whole tone scale — a series of six consecutive whole steps.

Wind instruments — any musical instrument whose sound is produced by the player's breath, or by the means of some type of bellows.

Woodwind — the orchestral family of instruments composed of flutes, oboes, clarinets, bassoons, and similar instruments.

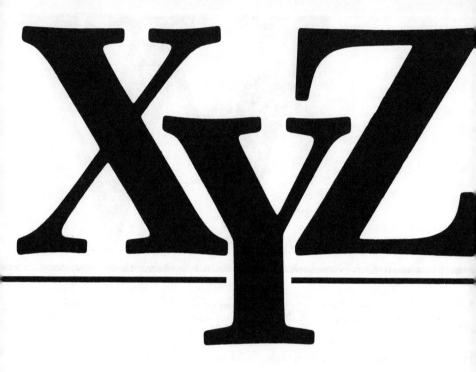

Xylophone — a percussion instrument which dates to very early times, consisting of wooden bars, tuned to the tones of the scale and struck with mallets.

Zither (Ger.) — a flat stringed instrument consistent of a shallow wooden sound box.

Mel Bay's
Manuscript Papers, Pads, & Books

Manuscript Paper (10 Staves—Highest Quality Paper)
Manuscript Paper (12 Staves—Highest Quality Paper)
Manuscript Pad (10 Staves)
Manuscript Pad (12 Staves)
Student Manuscript Pad (6 Staves)
Manuscript Book (12 Staves)
Manuscript Book (10 Staves—Wide Spacing)
Deluxe Manuscript Book (10 Staves)
Premium Manuscript Book (12 Staves—Highest Quality Paper)
Spiral Manuscript Book (12 Staves)
Deluxe Spiral Manuscript Book (10 Staves)
Premium Spiral Manuscript Book (12 Staves—Highest Quality Paper)
Student Manuscript Book (6 Staves)
Student Spiral Manuscript (5 Staves)
Chord Diagram Book
Guitar Tablature Book
Keyboard Manuscript Book
Student Chord Writing Book